D1239128

SNAKES ALIVE

Pythons

by Colleen Sexton

BLASTOFF! READERS

BELLWETHER MEDIA • MINNEAPOLIS, MN

Note to Librarians, Teachers, and Parents:

Blastoff! Readers are carefully developed by literacy experts and combine standards-based content with developmentally appropriate text.

Level 1 provides the most support through repetition of high-frequency words, light text, predictable sentence patterns, and strong visual support.

Level 2 offers early readers a bit more challenge through varied simple sentences, increased text load, and less repetition of high-frequency words.

Level 3 advances early-fluent readers toward fluency through increased text and concept load, less reliance on visuals, longer sentences, and more literary language.

Level 4 builds reading stamina by providing more text per page, increased use of punctuation, greater variation in sentence patterns, and increasingly challenging vocabulary.

Level 5 encourages children to move from "learning to read" to "reading to learn" by providing even more text, varied writing styles, and less familiar topics.

Whichever book is right for your reader, Blastoff! Readers are the perfect books to build confidence and encourage a love of reading that will last a lifetime!

This edition first published in 2010 by Bellwether Media, Inc.

No part of this publication may be reproduced in whole or in part without written permission of the publisher. For information regarding permission, write to Bellwether Media, Inc., Attention: Permissions Department, 5357 Penn Avenue South, Minneapolis, MN 55419.

Library of Congress Cataloging-in-Publication Data

Sexton, Colleen.
  Pythons / by Colleen Sexton.
    p. cm. – (Blastoff! readers. Snakes alive!)
  Summary: "Simple text and full-color photography introduce beginning readers to pythons. Developed by literacy experts for students in kindergarten through third grade"–Provided by publisher.
  Includes bibliographical references and index.
  ISBN 978-1-60014-318-2 (hardcover : alk. paper)
  1. Pythons–Juvenile literature. I. Title.
  QL666.O67S49 2010
  597.96'78–dc22

                    2009037593

010110   1149

Contents

Pythons are strong,
heavy snakes.
There are more than
25 kinds of pythons.
The smallest pythons
are about 2 feet
(0.6 meters) long.

Many pythons are much larger. The reticulated python can grow more than 30 feet (9 meters) long. It is the longest snake in the world!

Pythons have smooth **scales** that protect their bodies. The large scales on their bellies are called **scutes**.

scutes

Scutes help
pythons travel.
The scutes grab
on to the ground.
Strong muscles
pull on the scutes
to move pythons
forward.

= areas where pythons live

Pythons live in
warm parts of the
world. They live
in Africa, Asia,
and Australia.

Pythons are found in many **habitats**. These include **tropical rain forests**, deserts, and grasslands.

Pythons live in warm places to help control their **body temperature**.

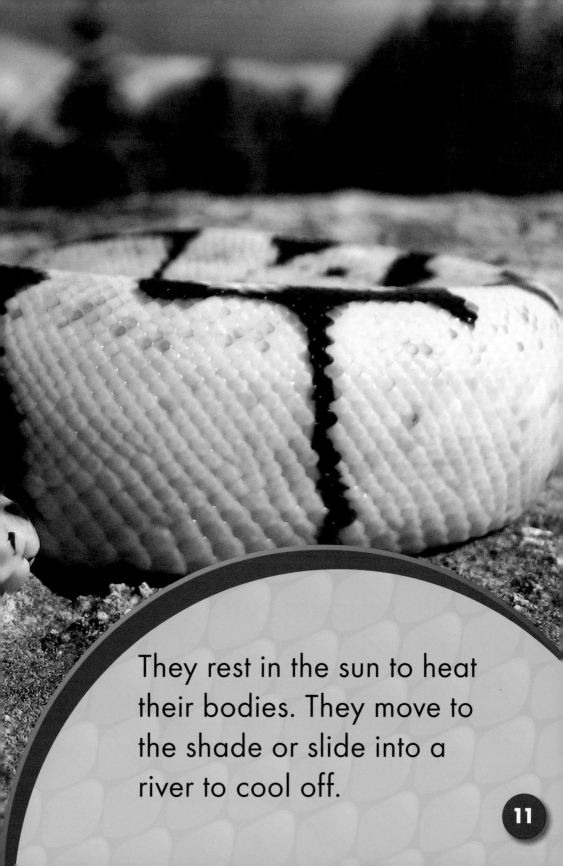

They rest in the sun to heat their bodies. They move to the shade or slide into a river to cool off.

Pythons use **camouflage** to hide. Most pythons have patterns of brown, yellow, white, gray, or black. They look like the ground around them.

Pythons that live in trees are green with patches of yellow and white. They look like the patterns sunlight makes when it shines through the trees.

antelope

Pythons hide when they hunt. Small pythons wait for lizards, rats, or birds. Large pythons wait for antelope, wild pigs, or other **prey**.

Pythons use sight and smell to hunt. They stick out their forked tongues to pick up the scent of prey.

pits

Some pythons have **pits** between the scales around their mouths. These pits sense heat.

They allow pythons to sense any animal that has a body temperature warmer than the air.

Pythons grab
prey with their
sharp, curved teeth.
They quickly wrap
their strong bodies
in **coils** around
the prey.

Pythons squeeze their prey tightly. Soon it cannot breathe and dies.

Pythons stretch their jaws open wide and swallow their prey whole!

Pythons can eat animals that are bigger than their heads. It can take hours to swallow a large animal!

Glossary

body temperature—the amount of heat in an animal's body; a snake has a body temperature that is the same as its surroundings.

camouflage—coloring and patterns that hide an animal by making it look like its surroundings

coils—loops; snakes can wind their bodies into coils.

habitat—the natural surroundings in which an animal lives

pits—areas of a snake's face that sense the body heat of an animal; pits tell a snake where an animal is and its size.

prey—an animal hunted by another animal for food

scales—small plates of skin that cover and protect a snake's body

scutes—large scales on the belly of a snake that are attached to muscles; snakes use scutes to move from place to place.

tropical rain forest—a thick jungle with tall trees where a lot of rain falls; tropical rain forests are in hot areas of the world near the equator.

To Learn More

AT THE LIBRARY

Cannon, Janell. *Verdi*. San Diego, Calif.: Harcourt Brace, 1997.

Gibbons, Gail. *Snakes*. New York, N.Y.: Holiday House, 2007.

Gunzi, Christiane. *The Best Book of Snakes*. New York, N.Y.: Kingfisher, 2003.

ON THE WEB

Learning more about pythons is as easy as 1, 2, 3.

1. Go to www.factsurfer.com.

2. Enter "pythons" into the search box.

3. Click the "Surf" button and you will see a list of related Web sites.

With factsurfer.com, finding more information is just a click away.

Index

The images in this book are reproduced through the courtesy of: Klein-Hubert/Kimballstock, front cover, pp. 13, 14-15; Allstair Berg, p. 4 (small); Robert Adrian Hillman, pp. 4-5; Frank B Yuwono, pp. 6-7; Yong Hian Lim, p. 7 (small); Jon Eppard, p. 8 (small); Emil Enchev/Alamy, pp. 8-9; Ryan M. Bolton, pp. 10-11; RLHambley, p. 12; Henk Bentlage, p. 14 (small); Serdar Yagci, p. 16; Santiago Fdez Fuentes, p. 17; F. Stuart Westmorland/Photo Researchers, Inc., p. 18 (small); Theo Allofs, pp. 18-19; McDonald Wildlife Photog./Animals Animals – Earth Scenes, pp. 20-21; Werner Bollmann, p. 21 (small).